The Lombards: The History and Legacy of the Germanic Group that Dominated Italy after the Fall of Rome

By Charles River Editors

A medieval depiction of Lombard historian Paul the Deacon

About Charles River Editors

Charles River Editors is a boutique digital publishing company, specializing in bringing history back to life with educational and engaging books on a wide range of topics. Keep up to date with our new and free offerings with this 5 second sign up on our weekly mailing list, and visit Our Kindle Author Page to see other recently published Kindle titles.

We make these books for you and always want to know our readers' opinions, so we encourage you to leave reviews and look forward to publishing new and exciting titles each week.

Introduction

A Lombard shield

The birth of Europe as people know it today was hardly an easy and effortless process. The continent was reshaped by centuries of continuous wars, raids, and the falls and rises of empires, and the most turbulent of these events happened at the beginning of the Middle Ages, from the 3rd-7th centuries CE. This was the time when the old slave society gave way to the feudal system that marked the latter Middle Ages, and it was also a period of battles between the Roman Empire and various nomadic groups. Rome waged wars, made and broke alliances, and bribed and negotiated with chieftains of various "barbarian" tribes to preserve the territorial integrity of their empire, but the razor-edge division between the civilized world of the Romans and that of the "savages" that threatened their borders was dulling with every decade. In fact, the constant need for army recruits swelled the Roman legions with barbarian *foederati*, a phenomenon that forced both the Romans and Byzantines to use a very subtle way of playing the barbarian tribes against each other via diplomatic schemes and bountiful rewards. A new religion was also taking root: Christianity became a reason for both unification and division, as different people adopted different variations of its teachings.

While many people are familiar with the Vandals' sack of Rome, the collapse of the Western Roman Empire, and the Byzantine Empire's attempt to reunify the entire Roman Empire, the history of Italy in the wake of Rome's fall is often overlooked. The late 5th century's political instability allowed wave after wave of semi-nomadic peoples, most of them ethnic Germans, to establish new kingdoms, only for most of them to collapse in an ongoing domino effect. Among the most important of these tribes to make an impact on Europe in the early part of the period were the Visigoths, Vandals, and Franks, which entered Western Europe and forged the earliest medieval kingdoms in Spain and France while battling with each other and Rome. Meanwhile, the Ostrogoths and

Lombards, despite entering the scene a bit later, left just as much of an impact on Europe further to the south.

Like the other Germanic tribes, the Lombards originated in Scandinavia before migrating slowly through central Europe, and as the Western Roman Empire collapsed and the Byzantine successor state in Constantinople attempted to reestablish order, the Lombards took advantage of the chaos and planted themselves firmly on Italian soil. From the late 6th century until the arrival of Charlemagne in the late 8th century, the Lombards were the masters of Italy, giving the land many of its modern names and adding a touch of Germanic culture to the overwhelmingly Mediterranean land. During their peak, the Lombards were one of the most powerful kingdoms of Europe and were approached by the Byzantines, Franks, and other European kingdoms for alliances and trade. The Lombards also fought with these groups quite frequently as they all contended for control of Italy and Rome, which at one point culminated with the Lombards even determining the election of one pope and indirectly exacerbating the schism of the Catholic and Eastern Orthodox denominations of Christianity.

Today, the Lombards are primarily just associated with northwestern Italy due to the eponymously named district in that country, but influence extended to most areas of medieval Italian culture, including law, economics, government, art, and architecture. *The Lombards: The History and Legacy of the Germanic Group that Dominated Italy after the Fall of Rome* chronicles how the Lombards established their medieval kingdom, the important events that took place in the region, and the Lombards' lasting legacy. Along with pictures depicting important people, places, and events, you will learn about the Lombards like never before.

Early Lombard History

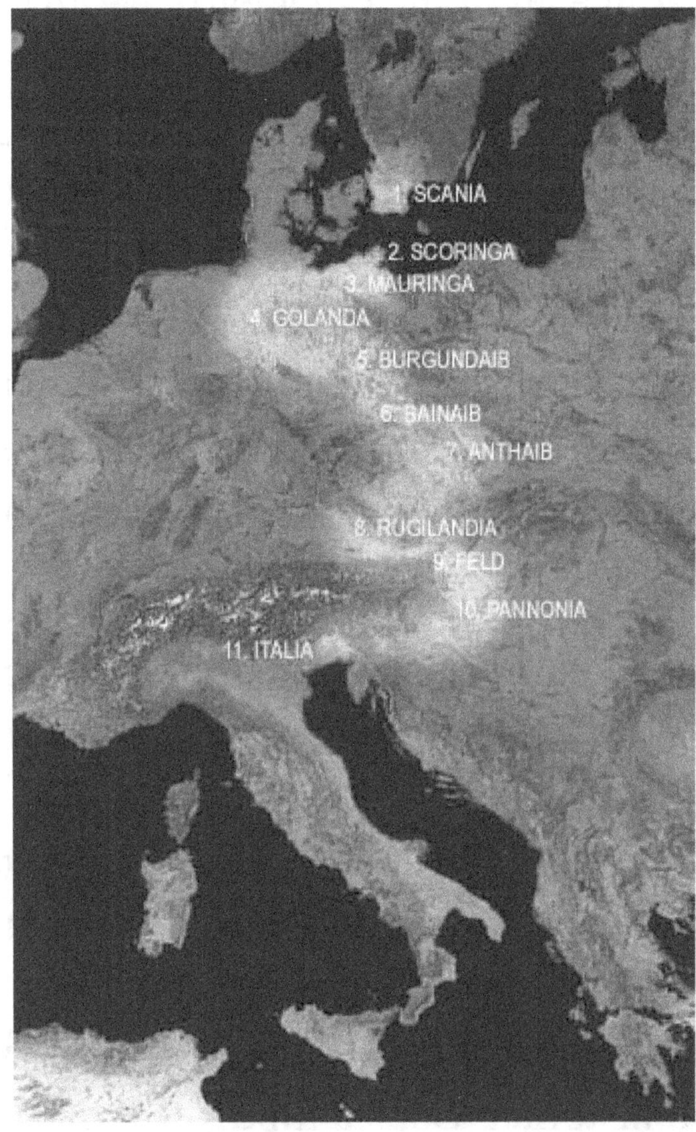

A map of the Lombards' migration

As with all of the Germanic peoples who flooded into Europe in the first few centuries of the Common Era, the early history of the Lombards is shrouded in mystery and legend. Much of what was later written about the Lombards during this period can only be partially corroborated by archaeology, and some passages are clearly more myth than history. Also, it is important to point out that like all of the other early Germanic peoples, the Lombards were not a fully literate society before they arrived in their final destination. Many of the Germanic peoples had a runic alphabet, but they never used it beyond some simple inscriptions, which meant they did not produce well-developed historiographical or religious texts. Due to the lack of written sources, modern historians have been left to piece together the early history of the Lombards from a variety of disparate sources.

  The early history of the Lombards was recorded in a number of different chronicles, and though some were written much later than the events described, many of them are still considered primary sources. The 6th century bishop and historian, Gregory of Tours, who wrote a history of the Franks up until his time, is a source for the Lombards since they were involved in various events with the Franks. The same is true of the 10th century Byzantine emperor and historian, Constantine VII Porphyrogenitus (r. 913-959), who wrote about the Lombards' interactions with the Byzantine Empire. Perhaps the most complete and accurate history of the Lombards was written by Paul the Deacon, a Church historian who was also a Lombard living in 7th century Italy. Paul's history of the Lombards is the most complete, although it focused more on Lombard activities in northern Italy and in Benevento

(Christie 1998, 74).

  In addition to these texts, archaeologists have unearthed
plenty of evidence about the early history of the Lombards
by tracing their movements in central Europe through
their material remains, particularly those left in burials.
Once the Lombards conquered Italy and became
Christians, they invested their resources in the
preservation of churches, cathedrals, monasteries, and
various other structures, which have been studied by
modern art historians. The combination of these modern
studies and techniques helps paint a more complete
picture of the Lombards' culture, chronology, and overall
impact on medieval Europe.

Giovanni Dall'Orto's picture of relics from a

Lombard grave

Modern academics almost entirely agree that most of the Germanic tribes flooding into Europe during the collapse of the Roman Empire originated in Scandinavia, even though details about their lives back home are more obscure. Scholars know a fair amount about these tribes after they began populating central Europe, in terms of their religion, political structure, and other cultural aspects, but whether they brought those ideas with them directly from Scandinavia or if they developed in continental Europe is open for debate.

According to Paul the Deacon, when the Lombards originally migrated from Scandinavia, they were known as the Winnili. He wrote, "In like manner also the race of Winnili, this is, of Langobards, which afterwards ruled prosperously in Italy, deducing its origin from the German peoples, came from the island which is called Scandinavia, although other causes of their emigration are also alleged." (Paul the Deacon, Book I, 1).

Paul's account continues to describe how the Winnili were led by two warrior brothers, Ibor and Aio, who served as leaders for the tribe, but not as kings: "Therefore that section to which fate had assigned the abandonment of their native soil and the search for foreign fields, after two leaders had been appointed over them, to wit: Ibor and Aio, who were brothers, in the bloom of youthful vigor and more eminent than the rest, said farewell to their own people, as well as their country, and set out upon their way to seek for lands where they might dwell and establish their abodes." (Paul the Deacon, Book I, 3).

It should be pointed out that while these two brothers may very well have been real, the accounts of them border on the mythical. Overall, the account should be read with a bit of skepticism because Paul wrote later in the account that Ibor and Aio only retired when the Lombards elected their first king about four centuries later, which is not humanly possible (Christie 1998, 13). The likely explanation is that Ibor and Aio were in fact great, early Lombard leaders and warriors who later became mythologized in the same way that Romulus was by the Romans. In other words, Ibor and Aio were Lombard national heroes, archetypes of how the Lombards saw themselves and their idealized, heroic origins.

It was during this early period of migration that the Lombards began making a name for themselves among the Romans and the other Germanic tribes, both on and off the battlefield. Winnili is a Latin term that the Romans used for the Lombards. The various Germanic tribes all had their own names, and those that became more influential later, such as the Lombards, became known by their German names, but the Romans initially had Latin designations for all of the German tribes they encountered east of the Rhine River and north of the Danube River. The Lombards likely never used the term Winnili themselves, just as few of the Germanic tribes of the era used the Roman designations of their tribes. According to Paul the Deacon, the Lombards were so known among the other Germans because of the long beards they wore: "It is certain, however, that the Langobards were afterwards so called on account of the length of their beards untouched by the knife, whereas at first they had been called Winnili; for according to their language 'lang' means 'long' and 'bart' 'beard.'" (Paul the Deacon I, 9).

By the time the Lombards became powerful in Italy, Winnili was a term that most of them probably no longer knew. Based on the primary source evidence, "Langobards" was apparently the term the Lombards used to refer to themselves, and it was also the term their non-Lombard contemporaries used, at least in many of the written accounts.

Paul the Deacon's account of the early wanderings of the Lombards provides some color to their background, but it is sparse in geographical details. The earliest movements of the Lombards are known through archaeological excavations, which indicate that they inhabited the Elbe River in Lower Saxony by the first century BC (Christie 1998, 6-7). The early Lombards lived in this region for some time before slowly migrating south into the Danube River valley, bordering the Roman Empire. The Lombards are mentioned in Roman accounts as one of the German tribes that attacked Roman territory in the Marcomannic Wars (166-180) during the rule of the Emperor Marcus Aurelius (r. 161-180), but they did not play a major role and were not mentioned again in Roman records until the 5th century (Bury 1967, 257-8).

Once the Lombards arrived on the Danube, though, the Romans were not the only people with whom they fought. The geopolitical situation in Europe was quite unstable by this time, despite the fact Rome had existed for nearly a thousand years.. A number of the Germanic tribes may have come together to fight the Romans in the Marcomannic Wars, but that was the exception, as they tended to fight each other more than anything. As more and more Germanic tribes began to fill the empty spaces of central Europe and push into the borders of Rome, non-Germanic peoples such as the Huns and the Slavs entered the picture from the east. For the Lombards, this meant that wherever they went, they had to fight for land and their very existence. They were more than likely a warrior-based culture when they left Scandinavia, but those values were reinforced as they fought their way through central Europe, because only a culture that valued warfare could survive in such an environment.

King Alboin

As they moved along the Danube River, the Lombards were eventually subjugated by another Germanic tribe known as the Heruls in 505. Little is known about this era of vassaldom, other than it did not last very long, as the Lombards overthrew the Heruls in 508 (Bury 1967, 258). The Lombards kept moving, though, through Bohemia into what is known as Pannonia (roughly equivalent with modern northwestern Hungary) in the mid-520s (Christie 1998, 31).

Once the Lombards arrived in Pannonia, it marked the beginning of a new chapter in their history. They came into more frequent contact, and conflict, with other peoples, including the Franks, Ostrogoths, Gepids, Avars, Slavs, and Byzantines. Pannonia was along the margins of the old Roman Empire and it was the northern reach of the Eastern Roman Empire, whose kings thought of themselves as the rightful Roman emperors after Rome fell. Although the Byzantine emperors ruled from Constantinople and their kingdom took on a Greek culture and ethnic character, they still considered themselves as the defenders of Rome and the Roman Church. Constantinople may have been their political capital, but they viewed Italy as theirs by right and still considered Rome to be their spiritual capital.

Byzantine Emperor Justinian I, who came to power in 527, was guided above all by the idea of the restoration of the Roman Empire, but to implement this ambitious plan Justinian had to subjugate the barbarian states that emerged from the ruins of the Western Roman Empire. The first to fall were the Vandals in 534. The Vandals had created a fleeting state in North Africa, but the restoration of the Roman slave system and the new taxes in the conquered provinces caused protest. Byzantine soldiers also became angry that the government did not provide them some of the conquered land for themselves. In 536, units in North Africa under Constantinople rebelled and joined local Barbary tribes and runaway slaves. Only in the mid-6th century did North Africa finally submit to the authority of the empire (Saris, 2006: 1-7).

Contemporary mosaic depicting Justinian I

Another victory was the conquest over the Ostrogothic state in Italy. After landing in Sicily during the summer of 535, the legendary General Belisarius quickly captured the island, crossed into southern Italy, and began the successful drive north. With the help of the Greco-Italian slave-owning aristocracy and the Orthodox clergy, Belisarius captured Rome in 536. That the Goths and Vandals were Arians in theology was no small matter either given the empire's issues with heresy. Arianism was so-called because it was named for a 3rd century

Egyptian Christian theologian named Arius. Arian theology was unique and controversial at the time because it asserted that while Jesus was the son of God, he was not one with God, which meant the Arians denied the Holy Trinity (Haugaard 1960, 252). Arian theology was considered heretical by the Roman Church and its followers were viewed as apostates, but it was popular with all the early Germanic tribes, especially those that lived along the Danube River in the mid-5th century (Christie 1998, 57).

However, since Justinian's forces acted as conquerors, the arrogance led to a widespread popular movement under Totila the Ostrogoth in 551-552. Totila was a talented military leader and visionary politician. As a representative of the Ostrogothic nobility, he was not willing to abolish slavery, but at the same time, he needed popular support against the far superior infantry of the Byzantines. Totila took into his army a group of escaped slaves and serfs and gave them freedom, and he also began to support free land tenure and private property in the Ostrogothic world. He even began to confiscate the estates of large Roman proprietors, especially those deemed to be sympathetic to the Byzantine empire. This provided him with the support of all sectors of the Italian population suffering from Justinian's imperial policy. Totila took Rome in 546 and soon conquered Greek-speaking Italy, Sicily, Sardinia and Corsica (Rosen, 2007: 137ff).

A medieval depiction of Totila

At the same time, Totila needed to be concerned with his rivals in the Ostrogothic nobility. Many noble Ostrogoths began to see their popular leader as too strong. Often,

Totila made concessions to the Ostrogothic and Italian nobility, thereby alienating them from the masses and causing them to lose supporters. In 552, Byzantium counter-attacked with a huge army commanded by Belisarius' successor, Narses, and in June of the same year, the battle of Tagin was lost by the Ostrogoths. Totila died in that battle, but resistance against the Byzantines remained consistent, and it was only in 555 that Italy was again part of a Roman empire (Rosen, 2007: 77-79).

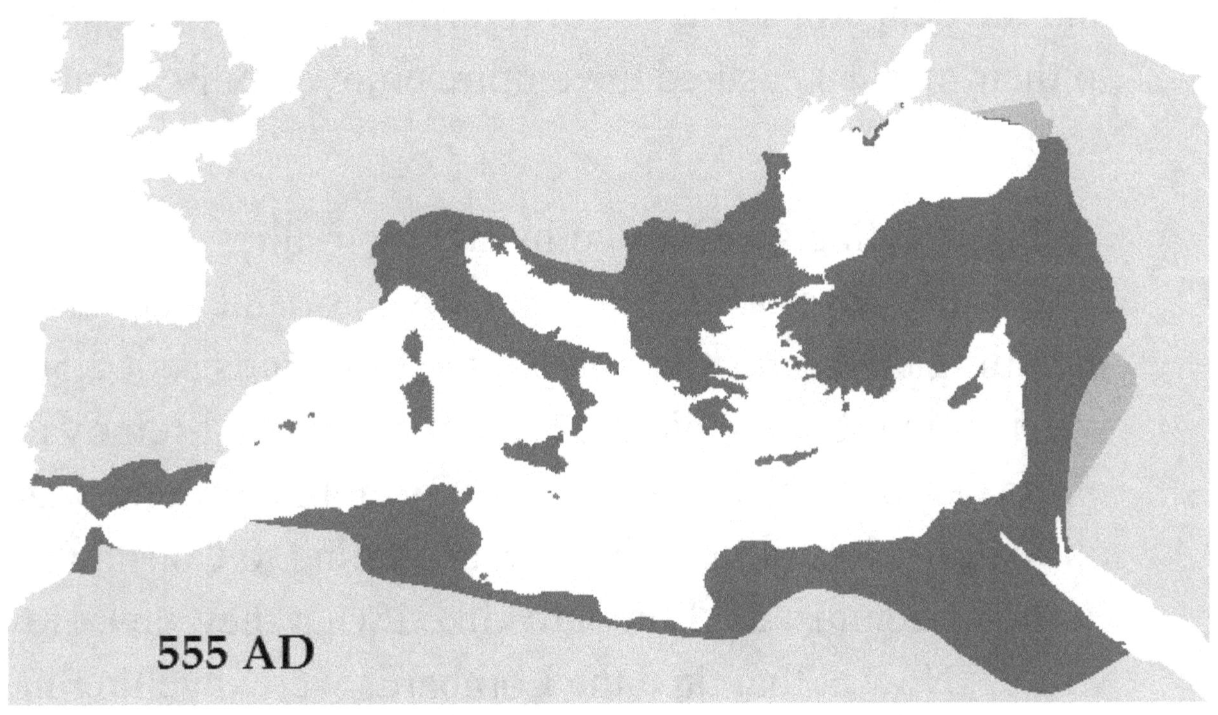

The extent of the Byzantine Empire in 555

Justinian tried to preserve the slaveholding relation in Italy and restore the Roman system of government. In 554, he issued a "Pragmatic Sanction" canceling all of Totila's reforms, and land previously confiscated from the slaveowning aristocracy was restored. Serfs and slaves who had gained their freedom were again brought into subjection. At the same time, Justinian began a war with the Visigoths in Spain, where he was able to capture a number of strongholds in the south-eastern part of the Iberian Peninsula. At this point, it seemed that the dream of Justinian's restoration of the Roman Empire was within reach. The problem was that the Byzantine administration did not understand the political world that created Totila, and the dangerous practice of returning newly freed slaves to their masters ensured the empire enjoyed only a fragile dominance.

While fighting the Ostrogoths and their allies, the Byzantines developed alliances with Germanic peoples, including the Lombards. In 552, the Lombards sent 2,500 warriors into Italy to aid the Byzantines in their removal of the Ostrogoths, and though the Byzantine Empire was ultimately successful in the war, according to Constantine Porphyrogenitus, the Lombards liked what they saw. He wrote, "Now at that time the Lombards were dwelling in Pannonia, where now the Turks live. And the patrician Narses sent to them fruits of all kinds and made them this declaration: 'Come hither and behold a land flowing with honey and milk, as the saying is, which, I think, God has none to surpass; and if it please you, settle in it, that you may call me blessed for the ages of ages.' The Lombards heard and obeyed and took their families and came to Beneventum. The inhabitants of the city of Beneventum did not allow them to come inside the city, and they settled outside the city, near the wall and by the river, where they built a small city, which for that reason is called Civita Nova, that is, New City, and it stands to this day. But they began to come inside the city also and into the church, and having by a stratagem gained the upper hand of the inhabitants of the city of Beneventum, they made away with them all and took possession of the city. For they carried swords inside their staves, and in the church they wheeled round and attacked all together and, as has been said, killed everyone. And thereafter they marched out and subdued all that land, both the province of Lombardy and Calabria and as far as Papia, except for Otranto and Gallipoli and Rassano and Naples and Gaeta and Sorrento and Amalfi." (Constantine Porphyrogenitus, Book XXVII, 30-53).

Though the account is mostly credible, it appears to conflate two different events. The Lombards first sent a relatively small force to aid the Byzantines against the Ostrogoths, which very well may have been accompanied by pillaging, but not long-term settlement. It was only a few years later, after the Lombards were more unified, that they entered Italy to permanently settle.

Although Paul the Deacon lists a number of Lombard

kings before Alboin (r. 560-572), Alboin was the first Lombard king to rule in Italy. The precise details concerning how and why the Lombards entered Italy remain open to debate, but the written documents seem to suggest that there were both pushing and pulling factors at work. Italy had long been coveted by Germanic tribes for its fertile soil, moderate climate, and relative riches, and the Germanic tribes also looked to Rome's guidance. In fact, nearly all of them wished to be "Romans," and German mercenaries had comprised the majority of Rome's army just before its fall. Thus, by the late 6th century, the Lombards were just the latest group to set their eyes on the land.

Other major factors that led to the Lombards leaving Pannonia were their neighbors. Pannonia was crowded with other tribes, namely the Germanic Gepids and the Asiatic Avars. Both of these tribes were extremely warlike, with the Avars being especially brutal in how they treated their enemies.

Alboin is remembered because he was a successful king, and he was successful because he knew when to use his mind and when to use his sword. After Justinian died in 565, the Avars and Gepids engaged each other in a war for control of Pannonia, which left Alboin and the Lombards in an advantageous position. After assessing both sides and determining who he believed would win the war, Alboin agreed to an alliance with the Avars against the Gepids in 567. The Lombards were the junior partner in the partnership, but once the war was waged, they were victorious, killing the Gepid king and then partaking in a most macabre ritual. Paul the Deacon explained, "But Alboin entered into a perpetual treaty with the Avars, who were first called Huns, and afterwards Avars, from the name of their own king. Then he set out for the war prepared by the Gepidae. . . Therefore battle is joined and they fight with all their might. The Langobards become the victors, raging against the Gepidae in such wrath that they reduce them to utter destruction, and out of an abundant multitude scarcely the messenger survives. In this battle Alboin killed Cunimund, and made out of his head, which he carried off, a drinking goblet." (Paul the Deacon, I, 27).

A late medieval depiction of Alboin

As it turned out, Pannonia was not big enough to contain the ambitions of both the Lombards and Avars. The historical texts state that the Lombards moved on to Italy under the condition that if they ever desired to return to Pannonia, the Avars would give them back their land. The reality is that once the Lombards left Pannonia, they likely never intended to return, as doing so would have meant conflict with the Avars.

As noted earlier, the Lombards first made an incursion into Italy during Justinian's rule, but in 568 or 569 they moved to the peninsula permanently, possibly invited to settle with *federate* status (Christie 1998, 62). In its final centuries of existence, the Roman Empire began giving federate status to Germanic tribes that the Romans could not defeat outright. The status usually involved the federate people being given land to settle in return for their loyalty and agreement not to attack the empire.

The Byzantines continued the policy to a lesser degree after 476, but with much less success. The Gothic War had depopulated large portions of Italy and destroyed much of the farmland, making the once fertile land a financial drain for the Byzantine rulers. It was apparently hoped that the Lombards would fill the role of the Ostrogoths, but that they would be more pliable than their Germanic predecessors. Byzantine Emperor Justin II (r. 565-574) made a major miscalculation in that respect, one of many poor political decisions the emperor made.

It is estimated that the Lombards entered Italy with as many as 150,000 people, which included entire families, among which were more than 80,000 fighting men. To all who witnessed the Lombards snaking their way through the mountain passes, it would have been clear that they were migrants and an invading army. Indeed, Alboin approached the move from a military perspective, and along with his own soldiers, Paul the Deacon wrote that Alboin employed more than 20,000 Saxon allies to accompany them on the trip: "But Alboin, being about to set out for Italy with the Langobards, asked aid from his old friends, the Saxons, that he might enter and take possession of so spacious a land with a larger number of followers. The Saxons came to him, more than 20,000 men, together with their wives and children, to proceed with him to Italy according to his desire." (Paul the Deacon, Book II, 6).

Once in northern Italy, it did not take long for the Lombards to leave their mark on the land. As much as the Byzantines may have hated the Ostrogoths, the latter kept Italy in order and prevented other Germanic tribes, or the Avars, from ravaging the home soil of the former Roman Empire. Once the Ostrogoths were eliminated, Justin II probably hoped that the Lombards would fill the political vacuum as loyal allies/subjects, but instead they immediately went on a rampage that was as bad as anything experienced in the Gothic War. Gregory of Tours noted, "Alboin, the King of the Langobards, who had married Chlothsind, the daughter of King Lothar [Clothar II], abandoned his own country and emigrated to Italy with all his Langobard people. They assembled their army and set off with their wives and children, for they intended to take up residence there. Once they had occupied the country, they wandered all over it for seven years, robbing the churches, killing the bishops and subjecting everything to their dominion." (Gregory of Tours, IV, 41).

A medieval depiction of Frankish King Chlothar II fighting the Lombards

This account is for the most part corroborated by Paul's, and while the details about what the Lombards did to the churches and bishops was clearly added by the Frankish bishop to paint them in a poor light, it was still probably true since the Lombards were Arians at the time. Since the Arians were considered apostates by the Roman Church, Gregory's account was also no doubt biased in that respect.

The passage points out the ease with which they were able to conquer northern Italy. It was once believed that the Lombards conquered northern Italy through superior martial prowess, but historians now think that it had more to do with the relative weakness of the Italians (Christie 1998, 79). The Gothic War had apparently decimated Italy so badly that the people were unable to defend themselves from the Lombards, and the relative lack of Byzantine presence on the peninsula at the time meant that they faced no true military opposition.

The Lombards wasted little time subduing the rural areas of northern Italy, as most of the natives were war weary and put up little resistance. The elites, though, who were invested in Byzantine success in Italy, put up a much stiffer fight. The Byzantine officials and the Italian elites fled to the walled castles and fortresses, many of them located in the mountains of northern Italy, forcing the Lombards to negotiate a surrender with the locals or lay siege. Paul the Deacon wrote, "The city of Ticinum (Pavia) at this time held out bravely, withstanding a siege more than three years, while the army of the Langobards remained close at hand on the western side. Meanwhile Alboin, after driving out the soldiers, took possession of everything as far as Tuscany except Rome and Ravenna and some other fortified places which were situated on the shore of the sea." (Paul the Deacon, Book II, 26).

It was no coincidence that Rome and Ravenna were the old seats of Roman power – Rome was surrounded by hills, and Ravenna was surrounded by marshes and the sea, making entry by land more difficult. The Lombards had virtually no presence on the water, but on land they were one of the most powerful forces in Europe.

Once the Lombards flooded northern Italy, they saw how nice the country was and decided to stay. At the height of their power, the Lombards ruled nearly all of Italy, with the exception of Rome, some major coastal cities, and Sicily. Most of southern Italy was ruled by semi-autonomous Lombard duchies, while most of northern Italy became the Lombard Kingdom. The Lombards were also greeted by a native Italian population that was largely indifferent to their presence and offered no notable resistance. To the native Italians, the Lombards were actually less brutal than the Ostrogoths, and their later rule was less onerous than that of the Byzantines. The Lombard Kingdom's first capital was the city of Verona, but it later moved to Milan before finally relocating to Pavia (Christie 1998, 145-7).

The Lombards may have entered Italy with a roar, but their rule proved to be fairly benign and tame compared to previous rulers. Gregory claimed that the Lombards massacred bishops and destroyed churches when they entered Italy, but once they became the rulers of Italy, the Arian Lombards were tolerant toward the Catholic population. The Lombards later converted to Catholicism, and they initiated a much lower tax burden than the

Ostrogoths and Byzantines, earning them the respect if not the love of the native Italian population (Christie 1998, 83). Furthermore, while the Lombards entered Italy as typical Germanic barbarians, they intended to stay as legitimate rulers, so they adopted many of the local customs and forged new relationships with the locals and other important kingdoms in the region.

Alboin was the driving force behind the rise of Lombard power in Europe and therefore can be considered a visionary leader, but he was also a tragic figure. He was known as a fearless warrior, a superb statesman, and a man with a long-range vision for his people, but he could do nothing to stop a domestic squabble from becoming lethal. Alboin was assassinated, which was nothing out of the ordinary for the time in Europe (and was actually quite common among the Lombards), but the assassin, or at least the person behind the assassination, was a bit out of the ordinary. According to both Paul the Deacon and Gregory of Tours, Alboin was assassinated by his wife, who happened to be the daughter of the Gepid king he killed in Pannonia.

Both accounts state that the assassination was a conspiracy, but the method used to kill the king differs. According to Gregory, Alboin was poisoned by his wife: "When his consort Chlothsind died Alboin married a second wife, a woman whose father he had only recently killed. She loathed her husband as a result, and was only waiting for an occasion to avenge the wrongs done to her father. In the end she poisoned her husband, for she had become enamoured of one of his servants." (Gregory of Tours, IV, 41).

Conversely, Paul the Deacon wrote that the king suffered a more heroic death befitting of a Lombard: "After this king had ruled in Italy three years and six months, he was slain by the treachery of his wife, and the cause of his murder was this: While he sat in merriment at a banquet at Verona longer than was proper, with the cup which he had made of the head of his father-in-law, king Cunimund, he ordered it to be given to the queen to drink wine, and he invited her to drink merrily with her father. . . Alboin suddenly aroused from sleep perceived the evil which threatened and reached his hand quickly for his sword, which, being tightly tied, he could not draw, yet he seized a foot-stool and defended himself with it for some time. But unfortunately alas! This most warlike and very brave man being of no account, and he who was most famous in war through the overthrow of so many enemies, perished by the scheme of one little woman." (Paul the Deacon, II, 28).

The Lombards Exert Their Power

The assassination could have proved just as fatal for the

Lombard people as it did for Alboin. Since they were the new power in Italy, Alboin's death could have opened the door for rebellion by the native Italians or invasion by the Byzantines or Franks, but the newly created Lombard dynasty proved to be enough of a stable state to survive the setback.

Alboin was succeeded by Clef (572-574), who did not rule long enough to leave any major impact on Italy. Following common Germanic tradition, Clef was elected as king of the Lombards (Christie 1998, 82), but little is known about his background. He too was assassinated while on the throne, but before he was killed, Clef managed to continue the "Lombardization" of Italy, especially in the north, by killing or exiling many of the remaining powerful Roman families (Bury 1967, 270).

After Clef's short rule, the Lombards had political and economic control over most of Italy, and they exerted complete control over the Lombard Kingdom and the duchies of Spoleto and Benevento. Interestingly, Clef's assassination did not lead to widespread political destabilization in Italy, nor were outsiders able to take advantage. The fighting among the Lombard dukes eventually gave way to a new king of the Lombards being elected.

Authari (r. 584-590) proved adept on many fronts, and

the 10-year interregnum period between Clef and Authari did not appear to hurt Lombard political unity or their rule over the native population in Italy. Rule by dukes was apparently a natural political structure for the Lombards, probably hearkening back to the way in which the numerous Lombard sub-tribes and clans existed in Pannonia and earlier. The idea of a unified Lombard state was basically foreign to the people, and therefore it was natural for their rule in Italy to be somewhat decentralized and fragmented. With that said, the Lombard Kingdom was always stronger with a single king, especially in the 7th century, when the Lombards faced repeated attacks from the Franks.

Like his predecessors, Authari was a warlike king who prided himself on using the sword to solve political disputes. Authari's most ambitious move was to lay siege to Rome, and although he was not able to conquer the ancient city, he did indirectly influence the course of the Church. Paul the Deacon explained, "Finally, after pope Benedict, Pelagius was ordained pontiff of the Roman church without the authority of the emperor, because the Langobards had besieged and surrounded Rome..." (Paul the Deacon, Book III, 20).

This passage is more important than Paul probably thought it was when he wrote it. As the passage indicates, the Byzantine emperors still played a major role in the election of the Roman popes in the late 6th century, but this event proved to be one of many that helped create the permanent separation between Roman Catholicism and Orthodox Christianity. The two would permanently separate in 1054 over a host of political, spiritual, and ritual differences, with this event proving to be one of the many that added to the schism. The Lombards were never able to gain direct control over Rome or the papacy, but they clearly began to wield more power over the Vatican, and in turn they slowly began to convert to Catholicism and were themselves influenced by the Church.

As the threat from Constantinople receded in the late 6th century, a new threat came from the north. After the Romans retreated from Gaul (modern France), the Merovingian Franks ultimately filled the cultural and political void. Descended from West Germanic tribes, the Franks had lived among the Romans for a much longer period than the Lombards and thus had more developed and stable political institutions by the late 6th century. By the time Authari came to power, the Franks had already interfered in Italian affairs, siding with the Ostrogoths in the Gothic War, and they were poised to do so again. The Frankish King Childebert II (r. 575-596) was a very active king, always looking to expand his realm through diplomatic marriage or conquest, and when he looked south to Italy, he decided to pursue the latter. Childebert II led two major campaigns into Italy in 576 and 584, and according to Gregory of Tours, Childebert defeated the Lombards and forced them to submit to his authority: "Next King Childebert marched into Italy. As soon as the Langobards heard of this, they submitted to his authority, for they were afraid that they might be cut to pieces by his troops. They gave him many gifts and promised to be his faithful subjects. . . Some years before he had received fifty thousand pieces of gold from the Emperor Maurice to rid Italy of the Langobards. When Maurice learned that Childebert had made peace with the Langobards, he asked for his money back; but Childebert was so sure of his power that he did not even send an answer." (Gregory of Tours, VI, 42).

As amusing as the account is, it is very telling of the political situation in Europe at the time. The Byzantine Empire was in an especially weak position, unable to dislodge the Lombards from Italy, which they believed rightfully belonged to them. The Franks, though, were in a much better position and able to play the Lombards and Byzantines against each other, even essentially stealing from the Byzantines with no fear of reprisal.

The Lombards likely did pay tribute to the stronger Franks, but the difference in strength between the two was probably relatively minor. The reality is that tribute payments were common in the Middle Ages and were often made to avoid an immediate war, allowing one side to bide their time while preparing for a future war. It seems that is exactly what the Lombards were doing, because when the Franks invaded Italy again at the end of the 580s, the Lombards were waiting. Paul the Deacon explained, "And without delay he dispatched his army into Italy for the subjugation of the Langobards. King Authari and the troops of the Langobards quickly went forth to meet him and fought bravely for their freedom. In that fight the Langobards won the victory; the Franks were vanquished by main force, many were captured, very many also escaped by flight and returned with difficulty to their own country." (Paul the Deacon, III, 29).

The Lombard victory was corroborated by Gregory of Tours' account, which provided more details, including the primary reason that precipitated the invasion: "King Childebert had received gifts from the Langobards, when they had come to ask if his sister could marry their King, and he had given his promise. When envoys arrived from the Visigoths, he promised her to them, recognizing them as a people converted to the Catholic faith. He also sent an embassy to the Emperor, undertaking now what he had failed to do before, that is to attack the Langobards and, with the Emperor's help, to drive them out of Italy. Next he sent his troops to occupy their lands. His military leaders marched into Italy at the head of an army and engaged the enemy. Our people were cut to pieces: quite a few were slain, some were captured, the remainder turned in flight and made their way home, but not without difficulty. The slaughter of the Frankish army was such that nothing like it could be remembered." (Gregory of Tours, IX, 25).

The Frankish military campaigns set the tone between the Franks and Lombards for the following 200 years. The Franks usually had the upper hand, but the Lombards more often successfully defended Italy from long-term Frankish occupation and were even able to conduct raids into Frankish territory.

The Franks were able to take advantage of the Lombards the most when they had weaker rulers, which was the case with King Agiluf (r. 590-616). Although Agiluf's rule was marked by a second period of conquest and expansion of the Lombard Kingdom, the first year of his rule was marked by rebellions, and the Franks tried to use that to their advantage. According to Paul the Deacon, Childebert ordered another invasion of Italy: "While the army of the Franks was wandering through Italy for three months and gaining no advantage – it could neither avenge itself upon its enemies, for the reason that they betook themselves to very strong places, nor could it reach the king from whom it might obtain retribution, since he had fortified himself within the city of Ticinum (Pavia) – the army, as we have said, having become ill from the unhealthiness of the climate and grievously oppressed with hunger, determined to go back home." (Paul the Deacon III, 31).

Gregory of Tours' account again corroborates Paul's, albeit from the perspective of the Franks: "When King Childebert received Grippo's report, he immediately ordered his troops to march into Italy, instructing twenty of his dukes to lead them in a war against the Langobards. . . They failed to capture the King and avenge themselves on him, for he was safe inside the walls of Pavia. As I have told you, the soldiers suffered very much from the heat and lacked proper food. In the end they turned homewards, having subjected to King Childebert's authority those parts which his father had held before him. . . Aptachar, the King of the Langobards, sent envoys to King Guntrum. 'It is our wish, noble King,' went the message, 'to be true and obedient to yourself and your people, as we were to your predecessors.'" (Gregory of Tours, X, 3).

It is unknown if Agilulf spoke those words to Guntrum, but it is probable. Agilulf had plenty of domestic problems to contend with, so it is likely that he would have had no problem paying Childebert a nominal fee in order to free up that flank.

In addition to fighting rebels and the Franks, Agilulf also

had to deal with the Byzantines on Italian soil. As mentioned earlier, when the Lombards flooded into Italy, they did not conquer the entire peninsula, so Rome and the major coastal cities remained in Byzantine hands and the narrow corridor from Rome to Ravenna isolated the Lombards in the south from the Lombard Kingdom (Christie 1998, 90). Although the Byzantine emperors who ruled after Justinian were characteristically weak and ineffective during the 7th century, the wealth of Constantinople allowed the Byzantines to put mercenaries on the battlefield against the Lombards. Moreover, the Byzantines could always combine with the Frankish threat from the north

In the mid-7th century, the Lombards had conquered most of the Italian peninsula and were able to focus some of their energies on internal affairs. It was during this period that Lombard culture came into its full bloom, particularly when it came to art, architecture, religion, and law. The Lombards built a number of impressive castles and palaces throughout Italy that were grand in design and purpose, serving as well-fortified citadels that could only be breached after lengthy and often costly sieges. Along with those impressive castles, the Lombards also constructed a number of churches and cathedrals in Italy, especially in the north, where many have been preserved for over a thousand years.

The Lombard Kingdom and Lombard culture in general began to reach its apex during the rule of Rothari (r. 636-652). Like his predecessors, Rothari was a true warrior king, conquering many of the remaining Byzantine territories in Italy, including the coastal province of Liguria, but what truly set him apart from his predecessors was the creation of a legal code. Written in Latin, the *Origo Gentis Langobardorum* was the first codified set of laws for the Lombards and one of the most important written documents in medieval European history (Christie 1998, 95).

Rothari's code was pretty standard in many ways, with a large share of it being dedicated to compensation for injuries, but it offered up a lot of information about the Lombards' past, including where they came from and what they still held close when it was written. Paul the Deacon wrote that the code was the culmination of oral tradition: "This king Rothari collected, in a series of writings, the laws of the Langobards which they were keeping in memory and custom, and he directed this code to be called the Edict." (Paul the Deacon, Book IV, 42).

Paul's explanation is important when one considers that in the 7th century, the Lombards' "barbarian past" was not so distant. For instance, the law code stated that if a man accused a woman of being a witch, he had to prove it in mutual combat against a male family member of the accused (Bury 1967, 287). The fact that the code had to make a provision to protect those accused of witchcraft implies that witchcraft was still a widespread practice by the Lombards in the 7th century and that many of the Lombards were still pagans. At the same time, the provision also indicates that the Lombard elites were consciously attempting to integrate themselves into the mainstream of medieval European culture at the time.

Rothari was succeeded by several kings who ruled for short periods, creating some instability in the royal house. The next notable king to come to power was Grimoald (r. 662-671), who waged successful military campaigns against the Byzantines, Franks, Slavs, and Avars. Grimoald was an ambitious king who perhaps understood the complex nature of geopolitics better than any of his predecessors. Desiring to incorporate the Duchy of Benevento into the Kingdom of the Lombards, but without waging war against fellow Lombards, Grimoald turned to the bellicose Avars to do the dirty work. Paul the Deacon explained, "Then Grimuald, unwilling to stir up civil war among the Langobards, sent word to the Cagan, king of the Avars, to come into Forum Julii with this army against duke Lupus and defeat him in war. . . When duke Lupus then had been killed there, the rest who had remained (alive) fortified themselves in strongholds. But the Avars, scouring all their territories, plundered or destroyed everything by fire. When they had done this for some days, word was sent them by Grimuald that they should now rest from their devastation. But they sent envoys to Grimuald saying that they would by no means give up Forum Julii, which they had conquered by their own arms." (Paul the Deacon, Book V, 19-20).

What Grimoald did next was impressive. Although he had a numerically smaller and weaker army than the Avars, he gave that illusion that it was much larger. Paul the Deacon continued, "Then Grimuald, compelled by necessity, began to collect an army that he might drive the Avars out of his territories. He set up therefore in the midst of the plain his camp and the place where he lodged the Avar (ambassadors), and since he had only a slender fragment of his army, he caused those he had to pass frequently during several days before the eyes of the envoys in different dress and furnished with various kinds of arms, as if a new army was constantly advancing. . . When the envoys of the Avars had seen and heard these things, and had repeated them to their king, he presently returned with all his army to his own kingdom." (Paul the Deacon, Book V, 21).

Grimoald subsequently gained possession of Beneventum when he married his son, Romoald, to Lupus's daughter, Theuderada, but as everything was going well for the king, he died in a hunting accident, leaving control of the kingdom to the boy Garibald (r. 671-672). Some ambitious Lombards took advantage of the young Garibald, and before long dissension developed within Italy. When Cunicpert (r. 679-700) came to the throne, it seemed as though order would finally be restored, but he was challenged by a Lombard noble named Alahis (r. 688-689), who briefly took power over the kingdom. Cunicpert was an able warrior and quite popular among his men, but Alahis was able to gather enough of the disaffected Lombard nobles to build an army to challenge the king. Paul the Deacon wrote that when the two armies finally met, the noble warrior Cunicpert challenged Alahis to mutual combat in order to spare the armies, but since he knew he would probably lose, Alahis denied the challenge: "Cunincpert dispatched a messenger to him, sending him word that he would engage with him in single combat; that there was no need of using up the army of either. To these words Alahis did not at all agree." (Paul the Deacon, Book V, 40).

Once the two armies engaged in battle, Alahis had the initial upper hand, but Cunicpert used some guile to gain the initiative. He dressed one of his men in his armor so that Alahis's men would focus all of their attention on him, and when the warrior wearing Cunicpert's army fell, Alahis thought he had won the day. Naturally, he was disheartened when he learned the truth. Paul the Deacon described the scene: "Then Cunincpert, seeing that his men had lost, straightway showed himself to them, and taking away their fear, strengthened their hearts to hope for victory. Again the lines of battle formed and on the one side Cunincpert, and on the other, Alahis made ready for the struggles of war. . . Then when the trumpets sounded, the lines of battle joined, and as neither side gave way, a very great slaughter was made of the people. At length the cruel tyrant Alahis perished, and Cunincpert with the help of the Lord obtained the victory." (Paul the Deacon, Book V, 41).

After Cunicpert took back the crown, some stability returned to the Kingdom of the Lombards. The next several kings were rather uninspiring, but they were able to keep the kingdom intact, and the Lombard duchies that had formed by the early 8th century in southern Italy actually helped add to the stability and ensure that a layer of Germanic culture would be spread across most of Italy.

Liutprand (r. 712-744) is considered by many to be the greatest of the Lombard kings, representing a bridge from the Lombards' Germanic past and their subsequent identity as medieval Italians. Liutprand was every bit the conquering warlord, but he was also a law giver, a devout Catholic, and a patron of the arts (Christie 1998, 102-4). Like his predecessor Rothari, Liutprand also commissioned a Latin language law code, but this one was overtly Catholic (Christie 1998, 113-4). A comparison of the two codes shows that Lombard Italy had evolved by Liutprand's rule and had no doubt been evolving for some time from an Arian Christian culture to a Roman Catholic society that was more closely integrated with the other major kingdoms of Western Europe.

The social structure of Italy had changed by Liutprand's rule, and so too had the Lombards, but they clung to their martial culture and their eternal rivalry with the Byzantine Empire. About midway through his reign, Liutprand embarked on an aggressive campaign to take even more land in Italy from the Byzantine Empire. The move came as Constantinople was being divided by the iconoclast movement, which gave Liutprand new opportunities to expand his kingdom. Paul the Deacon wrote, "At this time Liutprand besieged Ravenna and took Classis and destroyed it. Then Paul the patrician sent his men out of Ravenna to kill the Pope, but as the Langobards fought against them in defense of the Pope and as the Spoletans resisted them on the Salarian bridge as well as the Tuscan Langobards from other places, the design of the Ravenna people came to nought. . . Also king Liutprand attacked Feronianum (Fregnano), Mons Bellius (Monteveglio), Buxeta (Busseto) and Persiceta (San Giovanni in Persiceto), Bononia (Bologna) and the Pentapolis and the

Auximun (Osimo) fortresses of Emilia. And in like manner he then took possession of Sutrium (Sutri) but after some days it was again restored to the Romans." (Paul the Deacon, Book VI, 49).

Lombard Culture

Since the Lombards were among the last of the Germanic tribes to settle in Europe, they present a unique and somewhat more complete example of how these groups transitioned from pagan to Christian and from wandering "barbarians" into sedentary kingdoms. Eventually, as the Lombards established themselves throughout Italy, they merged with the natives and the Byzantines to form a medieval Italian culture, and at the core of that culture was religion.

The ancient Lombards, like all of their Germanic cousins, were polytheists who followed a religion very similar to the later Viking religion, which makes understanding it a bit easier for modern historians. Among the many gods and goddesses the Lombards worshipped, the most important were war gods, and although there are no written texts that document the rituals the Lombards followed, Paul the Deacon mentioned some of the religious beliefs they had during their early history. According to Paul, the Lombards believed that Wotan/Odin gave them victory over the Vandals, which led to them developing their unique hairstyle.

At this point, the men of old tell a silly story that the Wandals coming to Godan (Wotan) besought him for victory over the Winnili and that he answered that he would give the victory to those whom he saw first at sunrise; that then Gambara went to Frea (Freja) wife of Godan and asked for victory for the Winnili, and that Frea gave her counsel that the women of the Winnili should take down their hair and arrange it upon the face like a beard, and that in the early morning they should be present with their husbands and in like manner station themselves to be seen by Godan from the quarter in which he had been wont to look through his window toward the east. And so it was done. And when Godan saw them at sunrise he said: "Who are these long-beards?" And then Frea induced him to give victory to those to whom he had given the name. And thus Godan gave the victory to the Winnili. (Paul the Deacon I, 8).

The Lombards continued to follow their war gods until they came into more contact with Christians, and gradually converting to Christianity was a process that took hundreds of years. All the while, evidence from later periods in Lombard history demonstrates that they were tolerant of other religions, which may explain why they were also receptive to Christianity themselves.

The manner by which the Lombards became Christians is somewhat complex, though not unique among other Germanic peoples of the era. The areas of Europe closest to Rome converted to Christianity in the 5th century and then spread the religion north and east, with Irish Christians developing and proselytizing their own version of religion throughout the 6th century (Jotischky and Hall 2005, 22-23). The Church eventually gained hegemony over Western Europe through a combination of proselytization and marriage alliances, but the process was long and not without conflict. The area east of the Rhine River and north of the Danube River, which was German territory and never part of Rome, took especially long for the Catholics, and for that reason, most of the Germanic people, including the Lombards, were Arians.

The Lombards' conversion to Arianism had also been gradual, and they retained many of their pagan ways when they inhabited Pannonia. The Lombards were almost entirely Arian when they left Pannonia and entered Italy, which probably contributed to some of the hostility they had with the natives and Byzantines.

By Liutprand's rule, the Lombards were Roman Catholics, but much the same way as with other groups throughout Europe, it was a "top down" process. The nobles would convert first after having made diplomatic connections with other Europeans, and then a marriage between dynasties would be arranged, contingent upon the Lombard prince or king converting to the proper religion (Arianism in the pre-Italian period or Catholicism in Italy). The point at which the mass Lombard conversion began in earnest came when Authari married a Bavarian Roman Catholic princess in 589. Authari himself continued to identify as an Arian, which he probably only nominally followed to begin with, but their son and the future Lombard king, Adaloald (r. 616-626), was baptized in the Roman Church (Christie 1998, 185).

The Lombards' conversion may have been pragmatic and based mostly on politics, but economic realities also influenced conversion. The Lombard economy was part of the greater medieval European economy, which was based on market principles and barter. For the most part, the Lombard economy was based in the larger urban areas of Italy and was primarily conducted through bartering, while the rural districts of Italy were somewhat economically autonomous, although rents and taxes were collected from the noble Lombard landowners. That said, the Lombards also used coins, relying on a tradition that began in the ancient kingdom of Lydia in the late 7th century BCE. The Greeks and Romans used coins, and after Rome collapsed, medieval Europeans continued the tradition. In Lombard Italy, coins were used to pay rent, fines, taxes, and large payments, while smaller payments were usually done in-kind (Christie 1998, 141).

The Lombards minted unique coins in three zones – northern Italy, Tuscany, and Benevento – and used the previous Roman denominations (Christie 1998, 142). The quality of the coins ranged widely from mint to mint, even sometimes within mints, as there was no standard of weight or style set by the king or dukes.

Internal trade in Italy was certainly lively during Lombard rule, but the always ambitious Lombards eventually developed more far-flung networks with other peoples. The Byzantine Empire controlled coastal cities, which also continued to be economic centers even after the Lombards conquered a number of them. One of the most interesting and important of these Byzantine coastal cities was Venice, which would go on to become one of the most powerful city-states in medieval Europe thanks to its merchants. From an early point, the Lombards developed good relations with the merchants and leaders of Venice that proved to be economically beneficial for both. The Italian interior was wealthy in food and some textiles, which the Lombards traded to Venice in return for exotic goods that could be imported from around the Mediterranean (Brown 2001, 27). The influx of exotic goods from the Near East and beyond allowed the

Lombard elites to live lives of luxury that would have been impossible in Pannonia.

The Lombard kings also continued some Roman pastimes and luxury traditions in the interior cities of Milan and Verona, among other locations, by continuing to use the amphitheaters, forums, baths, and other intact facilities (Brown 2001, 26). By the 8th century, the outward trappings of Lombard culture resembled that of most of their Catholic neighbors.

However, the class division of Lombard society was very much a holdover from their time in Pannonia and earlier. An examination of the different legal codes mentioned earlier provided information about how the Lombards lived, but there have been disagreements among modern scholars pertaining to how the laws were applied to the different ethnic groups under Lombard rule. Most of the written laws focus on the Lombards, but the law applied to all, and the most important laws pertained to the worth of an individual, or his or her *weregeld*.

A person's *weregeld* was determined by his or her gender, socioeconomic class, and legal status, and as different as the concept may seem today, it was quite straightforward and beneficial to the stability of Lombard society. It may seem difficult to contemplate putting a tangible dollar amount, or in this case a *solidi* amount, on someone's life, but it was necessary at a time when the death or incapacity of a man could bring about the financial ruin of his entire family. The system thus served the dual purposes of compensating the family of any freeman protected by the *weregeld* and deterring transgressions against it. Within each class, there were several sub-classes that represented different values as well. For instance, lesser freemen were worth 150 *solidi,* while first class freemen were worth 300 *solidi* (Christie 1998, 117).

Lombard society was a patriarchal society, but women did have some rights. Like most pre-modern societies, Lombard women were legally dependent on their male kin, yet they were still afforded plenty of legal protections. The rape of a freewoman could result in a 900 *solidi* fine, and murder was 1,200 *solidi* (Christie 1998, 117-8). The typical Lombard freewoman fulfilled the role of wife and mother, but Lombard noblewomen had the opportunity to wield more influence. Due to their standing and prestige, Lombard noblewomen could fetch high dowries and play major roles in important marriage alliances, even if it was the men who made the final decisions on whether a woman would wed or not.

Lombard noblewomen, like their freewomen counterparts, were still under the protection and control of the men, and they may not have had the status that men did in the society, but they were still better off than slaves. Slavery was practiced by all of the Germanic tribes practiced, and it was also a system that the Romans employed, so when the Lombards conquered Italy, it was an institution that everyone in Italy understood well. Lombard slaves had no rights, but the owner could claim a *weregeld* if they were seriously injured or killed by a third party.

The slavery practiced by the Lombards was more similar to that practiced by the Romans than the chattel system used in the New World. For instance, even though slaves had no rights, they were frequently manumitted and would then be considered free or half-free (Christie 1998, 120). Paul the Deacon noted that the Lombards manumitted slaves from their earliest times: "Therefore the Langobards, coming at last into Mauringa, in order that they might increase the number of their warriors, confer liberty upon many whom they deliver from the yoke of bondage, and that the freedom of these may be regarded as established, they confirm it in their accustomed way by an arrow, uttering certain words of their country in confirmation of the fact." (Paul the Deacon I, 13).

The status of slaves also varied according to the relationship they had with their owners. For example, a freeman could marry one of his female slaves, but he had to free her upon doing so, while a freewoman was never allowed to marry a slave (Bury 1967, 282).

Along with the class divisions, it appears that the Lombard society was divided by ethnicity, and that there were two systems of laws, one Roman and one Lombard. Most historians think that the vast majority of non-Lombards were allowed to keep their status under Roman law, but that native nobles belonged to the class of Lombard freemen, which meant that they had to pay a tribute or tax based on the produce of their land. However, they were not required to give any of their land to the Lombard state (Bury 1967, 270-1).

By the middle of the 6th century, Italy had been thoroughly Lomardized in terms of its laws, with most of the important laws of the land, as well as the administrative institutions, being Lombard, not Roman (Bury 1967, 271). Rome had by that time long ceased to be a viable political entity and existed in name only. Rome's very political importance had long been transferred to Constantinople, although it still was an important ecclesiastical center and would later regain much of its political importance.

The most visible elements of Lombard culture include the phenomenal art and architecture that was created across Italy during their rule. Lombard castles in the north tended to be well-protected citadels, often located on or near a lake, while palaces in the south were also quite large and defensible, as they had to protect the dukes and the king when he came for visits. The Lombard duchies were only semi-autonomous, so whenever the king came to the duchy, the duke had to take care of him. Besides being waited on hand and foot, the dukes would entertain the king by bringing him on hunting expeditions (Christie 1998, 161). Once the king and the dukes were done with a long day of hunting, they would retire to the palace for a night of revelry and then go to Mass the following day to atone for their sins.

The churches of the Lombards were works of art themselves, but inside the churches, Lombard craftsmen revealed their best talents. Intricate designs of interwoven bands, with dragons and other mythological creatures occasionally mixed in, decorate wooden beams and walls throughout many Lombard churches (Christie 1998, 199). One Lombard queen, Theudelinde, who was the queen of Authari and then Agilulf, took a particular interest in the arts by dedicating the Church of St. John the Baptist in Monza, near Milan, and endowing it with copious amounts of gold and silver (Paul the Deacon, Book IV, 21). Theudelinda also had her own palace built where she commissioned a now lost mosaic that detailed the history of the Lombards. Paul the Deacon explained, "There also the aforesaid queen built herself a palace, in which she caused to be painted something of the achievements of the Langobards. In this painting it is clearly shown in what way the Langobards at the time cut their hair, and what was their dress and what their appearance. They shave the neck, and left it bare up to the back of the head, having their hair hanging down on the face as far as the mouth and parting it on either side by a part in the forehead. Their garments were loose and mostly linen, such as the Anglo-Saxons are wont to war, ornamented with broad borders woven in various colors. Their shoes, indeed, were open almost up to the tip of the great toe, and were held on by shoe latchets interlacing alternately. But later they began to wear trousers, over which they put leggings of shaggy woolen cloth when they rode. But they had taken that from a custom of the Romans." (Paul the Deacon IV, 22).

The Altar of King Ratchis

A picture of the inside of the Church of Santa Sofia in Benevento

A Lombard cross

Of course, the art and architecture that the Lombards would become known for would not have been possible without their aptitude for warfare, which comprised a major part of their culture. In some respects, Lombard warfare was similar to their Germanic contemporaries - the ancient Germans elected their kings from among a particular clan, and the king always had to be a warrior who had proven himself in battle (Bury 1967, 13). Even after the Lombards entered Italy and became a sedentary people and a part of the medieval European community, they often continued to elect their kings in this way when there was an unexpected vacancy. When it came to raiding and pillaging, the primary sources indicate that the

Lombards could be brutal, albeit no more brutal than the Ostrogoths or Franks (and less so than the Avars). Accounts of Lombard kings fashioning their enemies' skulls into drinking vessels may be shocking to modern readers, but that was a common occurrence throughout the Middle Ages.

Archaeological discoveries of Lombard gravesites along the Danube River reveal that the early Lombards were skilled at riding horses (Christie 1998, 7). This may not seem particularly interesting given that mounted knights played a large role in medieval European history, but the early Germanic tribes rarely fought on horseback, which makes the find and the Lombards potentially unique. And unlike some other Germanic tribes, particularly the Vandals, who developed naval fleets of varying size out of necessity, the Lombards never built a fleet (Bury 1967, 268). The Lombards' aversion to the sea was the primary factor that kept them from conquering all of Italy, as it was nearly impossible for armies to conquer Venice, Ravenna, and other cities that had the sea on one side and swamps around most land entrances.

The Decline of the Lombards

After Liutprand's long and relatively stable and productive rule, the Lombard Kingdom was living on borrowed time, with only five more kings to rule. The

Lombards were in many ways the victim of their own success, as they had built a successful, wealthy kingdom that was coveted by other powerful European kingdoms. By the mid-8th century, who those enemies were and what they wanted was no secret, so the Lombards were forced into a state of near constant warfare. It did not help that Rome, located in the middle of Italy and virtually an independent state at that point, was still the religious and political focal point of the Franks and Byzantines.

Despite the external pressure, the Lombards' decline began from within. Italy under the Lombards was a divided state, with the Lombard Kingdom in the north and the duchies of Benevento and Spoleto in the south. The Duke of Cividale in the north held a powerful position, though the land was technically part of the Lombard Kingdom. In theory, all of the Lombard duchies were subordinate to the kingdom, but this was not always the case in practice. The strong Lombard kings were able to keep the duchies under control, but during periods of discord, the southern duchies, which were separated from the north by a thin strip of Byzantine/papal land, had to manage affairs on their own.

That situation seems to have been the primary factor in the decline of the Lombard state, as evidenced by the law codes of Ratchis (r. 744-749; 756-757) and Aistulf (r. 749-756). Unlike the law codes of their predecessors, which depicted an orderly and well-regimented, if not violent kingdom, those of Ratchis and Aistulf depict the region as having lost its political homogeneity even more. Local dukes and princes asserted more power and autonomy, and there seemed to be little that the king or the primary dukes could do to stop the trend (Christie 1998, 114).

In conjunction with that, the internal divisions also made it difficult to fight powerful outsiders. As the Lombard dukes gained more power at the expense of the king, old rivals entered the scene to reclaim land. After the era of iconoclasm subsided in the Byzantine Empire in the late 8th century, the Byzantines were able to retake land in southern Italy from the Lombards and then use the coastal cities they held as beachheads to take back land in southern Italy.

Around the same time, the biggest threat to Lombard hegemony in Italy came from the north. The Franks had occasionally been allied with the Lombards, but more often than not they were rivals, and the confrontation came to a head in the late 8th century. With the establishment of the Merovingian Dynasty, the Franks became the rulers of Francia and the most powerful people in Western Europe, and when the Frankish prince Charles Martel established the Carolingian Dynasty, the Franks looked to Rome with greater desire and purpose.

Charles Martel's grandson, Charlemagne, conquered various Germanic peoples within his realm before turning his attention south to Rome. Charlemagne wanted more than anything to claim the title "Emperor of Rome," but there were a couple of obstacles standing in his way. The biggest obstacles were the Byzantines, who had claimed to be the true Roman emperors since the Western Roman Empire collapsed in 476. Charlemagne had dealt with the Byzantine Empire for most of his life and was not impressed. He knew that the Byzantines posed no real threat to France, and that if he wanted to claim the title of Roman Emperor, he only needed to be proclaimed so by the pope.

Reliquary of Charlemagne

To get to Rome, Charlemagne had to go through the Lombards, but he wasted little time leading his army south into Italy in 773. He besieged the Lombard cities of Pavia and Verona in 773-774, reducing both and claiming the kingship over the Lombards for himself (Christie 1998, 106). The last Lombard king before Charlemagne was Adelchis (759-774), who fled to Constantinople.

Knowing that uprooting the Lombard elites would be logistically difficult and would probably lead to enduring rebellions, Charlemagne decided to allow most of the dukes to keep their titles and land, and since Charlemagne did not campaign much south of Rome, the Duchy of Benevento remained independent (Christie 1998, 107-8).

It was no coincidence that Charlemagne kept the status quo in place. As he solidified his territories and continued to rule, he came to understand that, with so many different peoples and cultures within his kingdom, he needed to set up his government less like a homogeneous kingdom and more like an empire that demanded obedience and some standardization, even as it took differences of culture and language into account. He looked at the only great example he knew and began modeling his kingdom after Rome. For example, Charlemagne worked to make the royal court and his courtiers key players in government and politics, creating an impression of consensus. He also created annual assemblies at which the people were shown to be giving input into Royal decisions. The results of these assemblies were widely published, and key members of the Frankish people were also made into vassals, rewarding powerful individuals and stemming any possible dissent by folding them into the government itself. Envoys were also constantly set out to report back to Charlemagne on whether those under him were keeping their promises and doing their duties.

While it is undeniable that the coronation of Charlemagne as emperor in 800 was a major event, it highlighted something that had, in effect, already happened. Charlemagne knelt before the tomb of Saint Peter, on which rested the imperial crown of the Roman Empire, and as he rose, Pope Leo III slipped the crown on Charlemagne's head and knelt down in homage to Emperor Charlemagne (no pope before or since has done that). The multitude in St Peter's called out, "To Charles, the most pious Augustus, crowned by God, to our great and pacific emperor, life and victory."

***Imperial Coronation of Charlemagne*, by Friedrich Kaulbach**

When Charlemagne died in 814, he left an empire at the height of its power, with a solid foundation and a relatively young successor. That empire would fully disintegrate within 100 years, but it had permanently altered the trajectory of Europe's history and borders, and it all but broke the Lombards' power in Italy. Even after Charlemagne left southern Italy to the Lombards, they lost much of that land to the Byzantines, and the Normans arrived in the late 11th century. By 1077, the Duchy of Benevento had ceased to exist, marking the permanent end of Lombard influence in Europe (Christie 1998, 211).

Further Reading

Amorim, Carlos Eduardo G. (February 20, 2018a). "Understanding 6th-Century Barbarian Social Organization and Migration through Paleogenomics". 9 (3547). bioRxiv 10.1101/268250. doi:10.1101/268250. Retrieved March 13, 2020.

Amorim, Carlos Eduardo G. (September 11, 2018b). "Understanding 6th-century barbarian social organization and migration through paleogenomics". Nature Communications. Nature Research. 9 (3547): 3547. doi:10.1038/s41467-018-06024-4. PMC 6134036. PMID 30206220.

Bluhme, Friedrich (1868). Die Gens Langobardorum und ihre Herkunft, ...und ihre Sprache. Bonn: A.Marcus.

Brown, Thomas S. (2005). "Lombards". In Kazhdan, Alexander P. (ed.). The Oxford Dictionary of Byzantium. Oxford University Press. ISBN 9780195187922. Retrieved January 26, 2020.

Bruckner, Wilhelm (1895). Die Sprache der

Langobarden, Quellen und Forschungen zur Sprach- und Culturgeschichte der germanischen Völker, 75. Strassburg: Karl J. Trübner.

Christie, Neil (1995). The Lombards. Wiley. ISBN 0631182381.

Christie, Neil (2018a). "Lomvard Invasion Of Italy". In Nicholson, Oliver (ed.). The Oxford Dictionary of Late Antiquity. Oxford University Press. pp. 919–920. doi:10.1093/acref/9780198662778.001.0001. ISBN 9780191744457. Retrieved March 13, 2020.

Christie, Neil (2018b). "Lombards". In Nicholson, Oliver (ed.). The Oxford Dictionary of Late Antiquity. Oxford University Press. pp. 920–922. doi:10.1093/acref/9780198662778.001.0001. ISBN 9780191744457. Retrieved March 13, 2020.

Daim, Falko (2019). "The Longobards in Pannonia". Prima e dopo Alboino: sulle tracce dei Longobardi. Napoli: Guida. pp. 221–241.

Darvill, Timothy (2009). "Lombards". The Concise Oxford Dictionary of Archaeology (3 ed.). Oxford University Press. doi:10.1093/acref/9780199534043.001.0001. ISBN 9780191727139. Retrieved January 25, 2020.

Everett, Nicholas (2003). Literacy in Lombard Italy, c.

568-774. Cambridge: Cambridge University Press. ISBN 9780521819053.

Fröhlich, Hermann (1976). "Zur Herkunft der Langobarden". In Quellen und Forschungen aus italienischen Archiven und Bibliotheken (QFIAB) 55/56. Tübingen : Max Niemeyer. pp. 1–21.

Fröhlich, Hermann (1980). Studien zur langobardischen Thronfolge. In two volumes. Diss. Eberhard-Karls-Universität zu Tübingen.

Giess, Hildegard (September 1959). "The Sculpture of the Cloister of Santa Sofia in Benevento". The Art Bulletin. 41 (3): 249–256. JSTOR 3047841.

Grimm, Jacob (1875–78) [1st ed. 1835]. Deutsche Mythologie

Gwatkin, H. M., Whitney, J. P. (ed) (1913). The Cambridge Medieval History: Volume II—The Rise of the Saracens and the Foundations of the Western Empire.

Hallenbeck, Jan T. (1982). "Pavia and Rome: The Lombard Monarchy and the Papacy in the 8th century". Transactions of the American Philosophical Society. New Series. Philadelphia. 74 (4).

Hammerstein-Loxten, Wilhelm Freiherr von (1869). Die Bardengau. Hannover: Hahn'sche Buchhandlung.

Hartmann, Ludo Moritz. Geschichte Italiens im Mittelalter II Vol.

Hodgkin, Thomas. Italy and Her Invaders. Clarendon Press

Leonardi, Michela (September 6, 2018). "The female ancestor's tale: Long-term matrilineal continuity in a nonisolated region of Tuscany". American Journal of Physical Anthropology. Wiley. 167 (3): 497–506. bioRxiv 10.1101/268250. doi:10.1002/ajpa.23679. PMID 30187463.

Menghin, Wilifred. Die Langobarden / Geschichte und Archäologie. Theiss

O'Sullivan, Niall (September 9, 2018). "Ancient genome-wide analyses infer kinship structure in an Early Medieval Alemannic graveyard". Science Advances. American Association for the Advancement of Science. 4 (9): eaao1262. doi:10.1126/sciadv.aao1262. PMC 6124919. PMID 30191172.

Oman, Charles (1914) [1893] . The Dark Ages 476–918 (6th ed.). Periods of European History. London: Rivingtons.

Pohl, Walter and Erhart, Peter (2005). Die Langobarden : Herrschaft und Identität. Forschungen zur Geschichte des Mittelalters, 9. Wien: VÖAW.

Priester, Karin (2004). Geschichte der Langobarden: Gesellschaft – Kultur – Altagsleben. Stuttgart: Konrad Theiss.

The Lombard Laws. Translated by Katherine Fischer Drew. foreword by Edward Peters. Philadelphia: University of Pennsylvania Press. 1973. ISBN 0-8122-1055-7.

Santosuosso, Antonio (2004). Barbarians, Marauders, and Infidels: The Ways of Medieval Warfare. ISBN 0-8133-9153-9

Schmidt, Dr. Ludwig (1885). Zur Geschichte der Langobarden. Leipzig: Gustav Fock. Also in (1884) Älteste Geschichte der Langobarden. Ein Beitrag zur Geschichte der Völkerwanderung. Dissertation. Leipzig, Universität.

Todd, Malcolm (2004). The Early Germans. Wiley. ISBN 9781405117142.

Wegewitz, Willi. Das langobardische Brandgräberfeld von Putensen, Kreise Harburg

Wickham, Christopher (1998). "Aristocratic Power in Eighth-Century Lombard Italy". In Goffart, Walter A.; Murray, Alexander C. (eds.). After Rome's Fall: Narrators and Sources of Early Medieval History, Essays presented to Walter Goffart. Toronto: University of Toronto Press.

pp. 153–170. ISBN 0-8020-0779-1..

Wiese, Robert. Die älteste Geschichte der Langobarden

Zeuss, Kaspar. Die Deutschen und die Nachbarstämme

Carlo Troya, Giovanni Minervini (1852-1855) Codice diplomatico longobardo dal DLXVIII al DCCLXXIV: con note storiche, Napoli, Stamperia reale, 1855

Hutterer, Claus Jürgen (1999). "Langobardisch". Die Germanischen Sprachen. Wiesbaden: Albus. pp. 336–341. ISBN 3-928127-57-8.

Taviani-Carozzi, Huguette (2005). "Lombards". In Vauchez, André (ed.). Encyclopedia of the Middle Ages. James Clarke & Co. doi:10.1093/acref/9780227679319.001.0001. ISBN 9780195188172. Retrieved January 26, 2020.

Vai, Stefania (January 19, 2019). "A genetic perspective on Longobard-Era migrations". European Journal of Human Genetics. Nature Research. 27 (4): 647–656. doi:10.1038/s41431-018-0319-8. PMC 6460631. PMID 30651584.

Whitby, L. Michael (2012). "Lombards". In Hornblower, Simon; Spawforth, Antony; Eidinow, Esther (eds.). The Oxford Classical Dictionary (4 ed.). Oxford University Press. p. 857. doi:10.1093/acref/9780199545568.001.0001

Free Books by Charles River Editors

We have brand new titles available for free most days of the week. To see which of our titles are currently free, click on this link.

Discounted Books by Charles River Editors

We have titles at a discount price of just 99 cents everyday. To see which of our titles are currently 99 cents, click on this link.